Houses Architects Live In

Barbara Plumb

Houses

Architects Live In

A Studio Book · The Viking Press · New York

To MG
With thanks for so many kindnesses

ALSO BY BARBARA PLUMB

Young Designs in Living
Young Designs in Color

Copyright in all countries of the International
Copyright Union Barbara Plumb, 1977
All rights reserved
First published in 1977 by The Viking Press
625 Madison Avenue, New York, N.Y. 10022
Published simultaneously in Canada by
Penguin Books Canada Limited

Library of Congress Cataloging in Publication Data
Plumb, Barbara.
  Houses architects live in.
  (A Studio book)
  1. Architects—Homes and haunts. I. Title.
NA7195.A7P59 1977   728'.092'2 [B]   77-6350
ISBN 0-670-38038-5

Printed and bound in Japan by Dai Nippon

Introduction

Why should houses *architects* live in be singled out in a book? Of what significance are their precedent-setting designs to someone who quite possibly will never be able to afford a custom-designed house, or to someone with middle-of-the-road rather than avant-garde tastes? Simply this: architects' own houses generate many of the ideas that ultimately filter down to influence the spaces, color schemes, furnishings, and objects that you and I live with. Just in order to keep pace with what's going on in their field, architects must, at the very least, have a knowledge of the latest techniques in the building and finishing of houses, both inside and out; an awareness of the newest and best-designed furnishings on the market; and a familiarity with the design classics of the past. It is part of an architect's training, and sometimes even of his or her talent, to have a keen sensitivity to the relationships between space, scale, proportion, line, color, and texture.

Architects, unlike most of us, are willing to risk trying out experimental design concepts in the laboratories of their own houses. If these concepts work, practically and aesthetically, they eventually find their way, in one form or another, into the houses of the rest of us. Even if one could never conceive of actually living—day to day *and* with a family—in the same kind of environments that architects choose for themselves, their prin-

ciples of design and their color choices are eminently re-expressible in one's own preferred style. It is the inspiration, the freshness, and the originality that count.

Among the many strong points of architects' houses, possibly the most exciting and most special is their sense of space. It is literally architects' sixth sense, and what makes their dwellings worthy of study and, perhaps, emulation. Beautiful spaces are so important to the soul and sense of well-being of architects that they will sacrifice almost anything else in their budgets to find the money to pay for them. Soaring ceilings, jutting balconies, changes in level are not discretionary extras to architects but the very essence of what living is all about.

Where architects do have the ability to save money is by buying a difficult site that no one else wants and designing a house to fit into it. They are also particularly adept at giving an illusion of privacy, even when neighbors are no more than a few feet away. And they have a remarkable talent for situating houses in nature and creating a pleasing relationship to it through vistas from decks and skillfully placed windows.

Natural light is so cherished by architects that they find any means possible for bringing it into the interiors of their houses, including clerestories and skylights. And they are master ma-

5

gicians at those particular tricks of artificial lighting that make both a house and the people in it look as good as they possibly can. Most architects, having cut their professional teeth on Mies van der Rohe's famous dictum, "God is in the details," are fastidious about the choice of such often-overlooked appurtenances as hardware, and meticulous in their insistence on fine craftsmanship for built-in storage and seating. The unfailing eye of the architect is capable of seeing a large plant as a piece of sculpture, or a carpet as a space expander, flowing like a continuous sea over raised platforms and sunken sitting areas.

Architects' innate sense of scale and arrangement provides them with sensitive and proper answers to such questions as: What size chest or wall hanging relates to the proportions of a particular room? Where and how high should a painting be hung? What types and number of objects seem right; how many too busy?

Many architects have a certain natural sense of restraint and balance which shows up in their discreet selection and placement of furnishings and art. The textures they choose for their houses are rich and delightful, reflecting a love of books, a zest for carefully chosen objects, an affinity for natural materials like wood and wool. At their best, architects avoid the pretentiousness of false glamour and recognize the merit of informal or inexpensive designs with style.

Part of the mystique about architects that the general public perpetuates is that they find it both easy and satisfying to design their own houses. In fact, the reverse is often true. Architects may have terrific psychological problems designing for themselves. They fear that the world in general, and most particularly the critics, will judge their houses as the most perfect architectural statements they are capable of—the very essence of what they, as architects, believe personal environments should be. Fear of failure at such a pressuring challenge has blocked more than one architect from putting his or her ego and reputation so totally on the line. It is bitter medicine, indeed, for an architect to prove to be less than brilliant in the design of his or her own house, when he or she does not have the eccentricities or bad taste of the client to blame.

Conversely, an enormous psychological advantage most architects do have is that they know how they want to live. They feel confident about the kinds of spaces, layouts, colors, and furnishings that make them feel the most comfortable and the happiest. And whereas architects may not succeed in creating unique or great houses for themselves, they frequently do triumph in producing pleasing, livable environments—no small feat, considering how rarely it is accomplished with any measure of style and sensitivity.

When one starts surveying architects' own

6

houses, intriguing national differences emerge. The Americans, Canadians, and English in particular tend to be quiet in their taste, preferring white walls to emphasize art, people, and spaces; and monochromatic color palettes in harmony with nature. At the other end of the philosophical spectrum, the Italians have an appetite for flamboyancy and daring in their interiors. Their playfulness and verve—even when most outrageous—delight the eye in much the same way as a Fellini film, which shares similar characteristics.

The word "house," as it is used in the title of this book, is meant in the broadest sense of home, shelter, dwelling, residence. Under the umbrella of "house," apartments as well as new houses built from scratch and renovated old houses will be found.

During my years working as an editor of *Interiors* magazine, Home Editor of *The New York Times Magazine*, Architecture and Environment Editor of *American Home*, and currently as Living Consultant for *Vogue*, I have seen countless houses architects have designed for themselves. Why then have I selected this particular group of forty? Some of the houses attracted me because of their originality or quality or harmony; others seemed so pleasant and comfortable I wished I could move in the next day. All have a character that makes me feel I haven't experienced them dozens of times before; and all have interiors alive with ideas suitable for adaptation to all types of living situations—from tiny studio apartments to spacious converted barns. The emphasis in this book is not on dazzling architectural shells or structures but more on interior spaces for living, and the relationships of those spaces to one another and to their furnishings and appointments.

I have attempted to offer variety in the types of houses featured as well as in their geographical locations—and have had to leave out more than a few houses I particularly liked, because they were too similar to others. But when all is explained and attempted to be justified, I cannot deny that my selection remains a highly personal one. At the heart of it is what I find excellent and / or exciting even after my overexposure to hundreds of houses over more than a dozen years.

Neither the number of pictures chosen nor the images shown were allowed to be dictated by the architects. The final decision was always mine. I have tried to give all architects equal and fair treatment, and at the same time I have attempted to show the examples of their work that provide the most ideas for readers. And at bottom, of course, it is that bounty of ideas that is the architect's most special gift to the rest of us.

Paolo Leoni

The stunningly beautiful setting for Paolo Leoni's house is Ponza, an Italian island in the Mediterranean famous for the striking houses that cling to its ramparts and overlook the gentle curve of its port. Leoni reclaimed a house that had been begun seventy-five years ago but never finished, by restructuring it to suit his own needs. He dug extra rooms out of the rock on which it stood and added terraces, parapets, and stairs. Modern technology made his scheme feasible, despite the potential hazards of basementlike humidity. A coating of Fiberglas on both the reclaimed rock walls and the banquettes protects them from possible dampness.

1. The house burrows into the rocky hill like a cave. New terracing and walls, plus an outdoor cooking and eating area, give plenty of walking and lounging space to enjoy the sun and the spectacular views.

2. In the kitchen the rough texture of the natural rock walls and ceiling contrasts with the smoothness of the slatted wood cabinets and the sleek modernity of the appliances and fittings.

3. The unruly face of the rock has been smoothed to only a slight texturing in the living room. In the raised-platform living area and in the dining area below, banquettes and corner tables hewn out of the rock provide sitting and setting spaces. The artfully sculptured fireplace can be enjoyed from both the sitting and dining areas. A bold mixture of colors on the cushions breaks the monotone of white, as do the shapes and hues of baskets and pottery.

Photographs by Carla de Benedetti

8

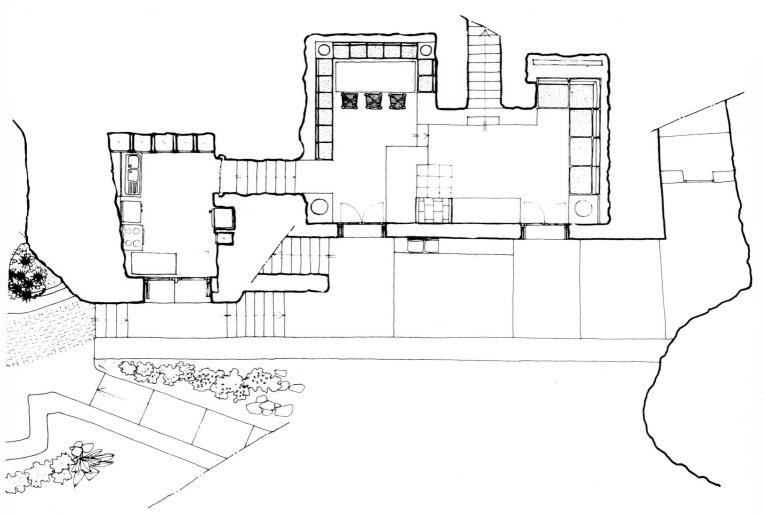

1

2

Rupprecht G. von Senger

In the Engadine valley in Switzerland, near Saint Moritz, a unique architecture stands out dramatically among the poorer Alpine buildings. Dating back to the sixteenth and seventeeth centuries, it is characterized by a richness, civility, and spatial grandeur born at the time of a flourishing Renaissance. Its stucco work and friezes look like Bavarian baroque decorations; its woodwork is in Tyrolese taste. Architect von Senger restored a deserted old house of this epoch, maintaining the original characteristics of the style while adding modern conveniences.

1. In the bedroom particularly fine wooden paneling sets off alcove sleeping areas.
2. In the entrance area thick plaster walls with a rough texture, wooden beams, and a stone floor suggest a rusticity that contrasts interestingly with the elegance and refinement of the wooden furniture
3. A large common room, which also serves as an extra living area, connects the various sleeping zones. Indirect lighting calls at-

tention to the finely wrought wooden panels on the ceiling. Both cabinets are local handwork. Leather and brass complement the paneled wood effectively.

4. In the living room vast white vaults create a strong and stunning architectural background for an exquisite mixture of art, modern furniture, and local cabinetwork.

Photographs by Carla de Benedetti

1 2

3

Gerolamo Gola

Memories of happy hours spent playing in the haylofts of his parents' farm north of Milan, Italy, suggested to Gerolamo Gola that he reconvert these special childhood spaces into a simple country house for himself and his wife. The upper hayloft, made into a large sleeping area, merges with the surrounding woods through a triangular expanse of glass. A rectilineal rhythm in the iron window frames echoes the ceiling-beam pattern. In the lower-level hayloft, which has been remodeled into a comfortable living room, an arc-shaped banquette and a fireplace bench provide seating. All the materials chosen throughout the house are rustic—fir and oak floors and ceilings, rough plaster walls, and rugged, durable cotton upholstery. What little furniture there is, is for the most part built in.

1. The sleeping area doubles as a second living space with built-in banquette beds along the walls. A lithograph by Miró hangs above one of them. Lamps are used like sculptures in the imposing beam-topped space.

2. An oversize masonry coffee table, in perfect scale with the imposingly large room, defines the outer edges of the second-floor sleeping area.

3. In the living room one long piece of built-in fireplace furniture incorporates storage, wood bin, and a seat. Glasses are grouped into a kind of sculpture on top. In contrast to all the brightly colored cushions and masonry, the walls are decorated with black-and-white photographs taken by the owners on their travels. Two multicolored hammocks are strung from the ceiling to supplement the seating.

Photographs by Carla de Benedetti

1

2

3

Carlo Santi

This tidy little house, nestled in a wood of chestnut, fir, and birch trees north of Milan, is simpleness itself, totally appropriate to, and in the spirit of, its natural surroundings. With steeply sloping roofs on the outside and matching ceilings inside, it has that protective, almost elemental character that seems endemic to compact structures. Natural fir walls and ceilings contrast crisply with white walls and fireplace.

Architect Carlo Santi divided the house into three basic parts: a room and bath for his three sons on the first floor, a living-dining-kitchen area, also on the first floor, and a second-floor balcony that serves as a combined master bedroom and work area. This open sleeping balcony is reached by a metal ladder that hugs the wall when not in use, or can be slanted out into the room to facilitate climbing. The furniture, consisting of safari chairs, folding chairs, and built-in beds with drawers and desks, while minimal, is totally in keeping with the rustic style of the house.

1. The kitchen, with its quarry-tile floors, brightly colored tile backsplash, and natural wooden cabinets, makes a pleasant backdrop for dining. Folding chairs can easily be moved out of the way to give more room for cooking. The stove, small refrigerator, and sink, ideally sized for the tiny space, fit neatly under a counter.

2. In the sleeping balcony, beds are placed at angles and mounted on top of drawers of different heights, to fit the slope of the ceiling. One long wooden shelf-desk overhangs the living area, a neat finishing detail for the white walls.

3. The fireplace, open on two sides to give off maximum warmth, is supplemented by an adjacent kerosene stove. It is used in the winter but screened during the summer with wooden panels. The black metal ladder to the sleeping balcony is so handsomely detailed and scaled that it looks like a piece of sculpture against the white wall.

Photographs by Carla de Benedetti

1

2

Giancarlo Bicocchi

With little more than paint, this old barn in Follonica, Tuscany, has been converted into a vacation house for Giancarlo Bicocchi and his family of five children. The architect had such a healthy respect for the integrity of the old building that he left the wooden beams and sloping ceilings as they were and just added new bathrooms and a kitchen. He painted the old floors with white road paint and whitened the walls and ceilings with lime. To contrast with this bleached background he chose the traditional colors that the Tuscan peasants use for their houses: yellow, red, and blue.

The ground floor, once used for storing produce, he kept as it was, and turned it over to the children for their games. The furniture is minimal—transparent inflatable plastic chairs, some simple modern pieces, and a few country antiques. The floor lamps, merely globes covered with colored cloth, give a warm and cozy atmosphere to the house at night.

The exterior of the house was left untouched, with the surrounding garden remaining one vast expanse of corn. The old threshing area directly in front of the house makes an ideal play space for the children.

1. An old door with its original hardware becomes a bright red exclamation point at the end of a white corridor punctuated with chrome yellow doors. The corridor leads into the living room, where the yellow of the hall is repeated in a large wooden coffee table and in a print on the wall which brings together all the colors in the house.

2. In the bedroom a fresh, summery look is achieved by combining a dark blue wardrobe and lighter blue walls with yellow shutters, a yellow door, and a yellow metal bedstead.

3. The theme colors of the house are expressed in the kitchen in pots and pans and cups hung from a wooden lattice of narrow slats. One wall is painted a deep navy blue for contrast.

4. The spareness and lack of clutter in the

living room make it easy to maintain and keep tidy even with five young children using it. The light-balls are placed randomly about, like playful sculptures.

Photographs by Carla de Benedetti

25

1

2

3

Winthrop Faulkner

When Winthrop Faulkner acquired a fine old stone barn near Middleburg, Virginia, his primary goal in renovating it was to preserve its original qualities, in terms of both spaces and materials. He left the massive oak, pine, and walnut beams exposed, but sprayed the high ceilings with urethane foam and painted them white. The walls are alternatively of barn siding or plastered with a white sand finish; he planed and sanded the pine floors, which had boards often as wide as eighteen to twenty-four inches.

The living areas and the kitchen—dining room Mr. Faulkner located in the second-floor hayloft because of the stunning spaces and the panoramic view of about sixty miles of the Blue Ridge Mountains. On the first floor, which used to have stalls and an earth floor, he installed a master bedroom with its own balcony, and two dormitory rooms. A concrete silo shades the balconies and windows facing west, the direction of the primary view.

The fireplace and bookcase wall, forming a low partition between the living room and the kitchen—dining room, does not intrude on the sweep of the vast space surrounding it but, instead, accentuates it by the contrast in scale. The landing, converted into an extra sitting room with a balcony of its own, becomes particularly useful when parents and children entertain separate sets of friends.

In furnishing the house, Jeanne Faulkner, an interior designer, worked on the principle that the huge space was so flexible that it could graciously absorb a variety of furniture periods and styles, from highly sophisticated to elementally primitive.

1. The exposed floor structure forming the rugged ceiling of the master bedroom contrasts effectively with the sleek modern furnishings and fabrics. Sliding glass doors open to a balcony with a view of the Blue Ridge Mountains.

2. Barn siding on two walls of the living room gives an impression of coziness without fettering the generous upward expanse of the space. An old painted horse from a merry-go-round is mounted above the siding. Simple cone-shaped Danish lamps hang down from the rafters. Antiques, modern classics, and comfortable seating pieces combine in livable harmony.

3. Natural wood on walls, floors, counters, and cabinets adds warmth to the dining—kitchen area. Mexican tiles, candlesticks, and Portuguese plates contrast pleasantly in texture and color.

4. The second-floor living area, divided into living room, kitchen—dining room behind the library-fireplace partition, and an extra sitting room on the landing, flows together as one grand space. A brilliant red hanging at the top of the stairs provides a bright splash of color as a foil for the subdued natural hues surrounding it.

Photographs by Norman McGrath

1

2

3

Antoine Predock

Tired of commuting to the city from the suburbs, Antoine Predock scoured the old section of Albuquerque, New Mexico, for suitable office space within walking distance of a pleasant one-family house. When he found an abandoned warehouse right next door to a run-down vacant house, his dream approached reality. He decided to make one inward-looking complex out of his acquisitions by enclosing both buildings with walls and giving each its own separate but connecting patio. The walls provide enough privacy from the street so that curtains never have to be pulled except for shade. Mr. Predock gutted the entire house, with the exception of the original bearing walls, to obtain a twenty-six-foot-high-ceiling sweep for the living room. A space-saving staircase winds up to an open loft area, formerly an enclosed attic, which accommodates the master bedroom, bath, and study. The continuous loft area contrasts with the first floor, which is divided into individual rooms. A children's wing on the lower floor can be sealed off acoustically from the adult zones of the house by a sound lock.

1. Mr. Predock reshaped the fireplace in the living room, adding stucco to re-contour its outlines. An old cabinet in the dining room was painted ocher and given a new laminated plastic top. An unadorned globe light makes a simple counterpoint to the classic lines of the Saarinen table and chairs.
2. The sleeping section of the open master bedroom can be curtained off for privacy and quiet. A railing of redwood and tempered glass leaves the area visually unobstructed. Through a sliding door a balcony for sunning or scanning the mountains is accessible to the bedroom.
3. A back porch area was incorporated into the kitchen to make it particularly spacious and airy. A gold vinyl floor and gold Formica counter tops complement the natural birch plywood cabinets, making the kitchen very bright and cheerful. Lighting is built in under all the cabinets.

4. Eliminating the attic made it possible for the ceiling line of the living room, previously three rooms, to rise to twenty-six feet at its apex. The handsome ceiling is redwood, which contrasts effectively with white walls sprayed with a sand finish. A light track provides illumination.

Photographs by Glen Allison

33

1

2

3

Allan and Barbara Anderson

A house that is custom designed but inexpensive to build—eight dollars a square foot —may seem too much to hope for, but Allan and Barbara Anderson, both architects, managed it through ingenuity and hard work. In Rye, an easy commute from New York City, they found a spectacular two-and-a-quarter-acre site covered with oaks, blueberry bushes, and azaleas—overlooking Mead Pond. The land, of which one third was under water, one third right-of-way, and one third a thirty-foot-high rock outcropping, had languished on the market for years at a bargain price because it was considered unbuildable.

Not to the Andersons, however. They designed their 2,000-square-foot house as three oversize sheds that follow the rock down the hill. A shingled exterior fits in with other shingled houses in the neighborhood. Six decks are vantage points for enjoying the landscape, which, though right in the middle of suburbia, seems like a woodland retreat.

To save money the Andersons decided to build the house themselves on weekends and vacations, with help from their friends. They called on professionals only to install the plumbing, wiring, and glass. Because the site was inaccessible to construction equipment, all excavation work was done with pick, shovel, and jackhammer. To avoid needless marring of the terrain, and also for economy's sake, the house was pinned directly to the rock. It took five months to secure the foundations to the rock; nine months for framing, sheathing, and shingling; and three months to install windows and doors. Then the Andersons moved in and started painting, tiling, and finishing floors.

Although Mr. Anderson's father is a carpenter to whom they could turn for advice, the Andersons solved most problems themselves simply by reading the instructions that accompanied building materials. Although much had to be accomplished through trial and error, when the house was finished the Andersons had mastered all the basic building crafts and skills.

1. High windows in the master bedroom bring in light with no loss of privacy. An angular doorway opens onto a small deck. The bed, covered with a bright orange spread, fits into a storage niche. The ceiling is natural red cedar.

2. An open kitchen is conveniently situated in the center of things, with ready access to the dining room and a deck.

3. A glass-enclosed tub-shower with a sauna above it is reflected in the master-bathroom wall mirror. The sauna wall is angled out to provide more interior space. From the top level a bather may gaze through the windows at Mead Pond.

4. The Andersons designed and made the long curved sofa in the living room. Stock glass doors open onto a small deck with a shingled railing.

5. The island kitchen, which has a view of the trees and pond, floats in the barnlike space between the living room and dining room.

37

1

2

3

4

Wendell Lovett

A small rustic vacation hideaway that would contrast dramatically with his large, sophisticated Bellevue, Washington, house was what Wendell Lovett envisioned when he bought a waterside acre of land and beach on Crane Island, in the San Juan Islands between Washington and Vancouver Island. He designed what he termed "a glorified tent with a platform" for a site covered with tall firs, cedar, hemlock, madroña, and maple, and built it himself with only one paid helper, working weekends for two summers.

The structure is suspended from two huge, triangular, inverted fir trusses that extend from the roof peak to the beginning and end of a deck, cantilevered eighteen feet beyond the concrete foundation wall. Glass wraps around three sides so views of the trees can be enjoyed. For economy and ease of maintenance, nearly half the structure is decked; instead of bedrooms, there is a sleeping loft.

Walls of red cedar boards mounted diagonally follow the thrust and slope of

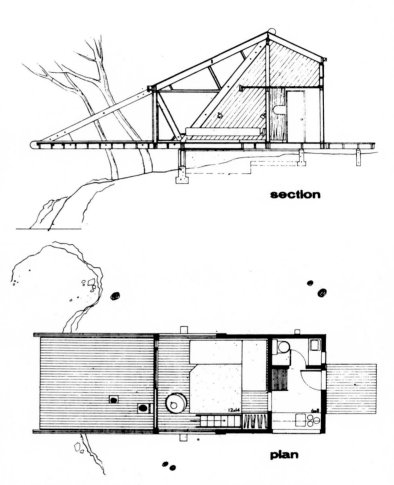

section

plan

the trusses, as does a ship's ladder leading up to the sleeping loft. Because the house is so small—only 370 square feet—furniture is kept to the minimum and supplemented with chairs from the deck when needed. Cotton-covered foam-rubber mattresses, which double as seating, sleep two downstairs; the loft has room for four. "The inside is just a place to come in by the fire in the evening and a place to sleep," Mr. Lovett says.

1. Decking continues into the living room and the kitchen. Storage cupboards are decorated with Lovett supergraphics. Lots of pillows and skins turn the sleeping mattresses into comfortable places to sit. The door leads to the kitchen; up the ship's ladder to the right is the sleeping loft.

2. The recessed floor encourages easy lounging on the deck around the Lovett-designed free-standing metal fireplace—"Like sitting on a log at the beach." A marine chart of Crane and its surrounding islands is mounted on an orange panel that screens the interior from a neighboring house.

3. On the east wall of the house can be seen the supports of the cantilevered deck, the irregular side windows, and the horizontal kitchen window.

Photographs by Chris Staub

1

2   3

Arthur Erickson

It was the *placement* of a garage and small storage building—not their architectural design or layout—that convinced Arthur Erickson that he had to have them for his own. Because the buildings were situated right on the lane (the owners were hoping one day to build a large house in the center of their property), all the rest of the land was a garden. Mr. Erickson contoured the lot, located in Vancouver, British Columbia, to obscure a view of a neighboring house; put in a pool with a marble peninsula; made a brick terrace; added a fish pond and planted ornamental grasses, rhododendron, pine, azalea, mountain laurel, and dogwood. He wanted the garden to seem unkempt and rampant "like a forest clearing in some indefinable wilderness."

The garage accommodates the living room; the storage building holds a bedroom-studio; a dining area with a cupboard-kitchen along one wall links the two. Vaulted skylights of clear Plexiglas in the dining area and the bathroom are surrounded by planting troughs that bring the green of the trees overhead into the rooms. A small greenhouse on the end of the studio completes the total integration of the house with plants and nature.

As a counterpoint to the freshness and abundance of the greenery, the interior of the house is finished sparely but in the most sophisticated manner with the richest possible materials—suedes, velvets, and silks. The contrast between the nature outside and the highly civilized manmade environment inside allows for the greatest possible variety and interest within the confines of a property measuring only 66 by 120 feet.

1. The luxurious bathroom, with a teak dresser built in along one wall, also serves as a dressing room. Sunlight pours through a vaulted skylight edged with a planting trough. The walls are covered with Italian leather. The shower is molded Fiberglas.
2. The kitchen is in the dining area, hidden behind floor-to-ceiling teak doors. In a niche

opposite is a serving counter. Overhead is a vaulted Fiberglas skylight bedecked with plants. The floors are terrazzo. At the far end of the room is a studio with walls sheathed with mirrors and yellow Thai silk. To the right is a greenhouse and to the left (not shown) a bed loft with a skylight.

3. The garden has been built up at the far end to screen a neighboring house. A marble slab juts into a pool, thick with lily pads and ornamental grasses; a brick terrace borders the pool.

4. The living room, with a view of the garden through floor-to-ceiling windows, is opulently furnished with a Chinese carpet and beige velvet Italian furniture. Walls are covered in beige Italian kid suede; the curtains are white Thai silk. Cove lighting washes one wall.

5. One end of the studio has been arranged as a corner for contemplation, with a Le Corbusier chaise overlooking the adjoining greenhouse and the pool beyond.

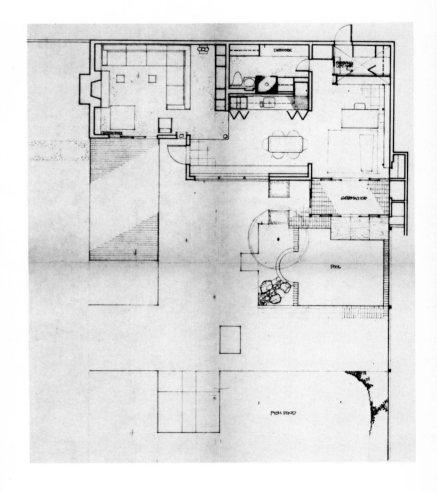

Photographs by Simon Scott

1

2

3

4

5

Luis Barragan

"No architecture is so haughty as that which is simple," wrote John Ruskin. If any house demonstrates the truth of this observation, it is Luis Barragan's in Mexico City. Here the power of simple but strong forms, the excitement of strong colors, and the richness of natural textures combine to make one of the notable classics of modern design.

Located on a quiet street in a working-class neighborhood, it appears windowless, warehouse-like, totally anonymous on the outside. But inside, an enormous living room overlooks a wild and romantic garden through one large glass opening, ten feet square, set flush into heavy concrete walls. Massive rough plaster walls, in white or vivid colors, are a striking counterpoint to the openness of the soaring fifteen-foot beamed ceilings. Partitions, low enough not to obstruct the light or the free flow of space, divide the living room into a sitting area, a library, and a work area.

The play of natural light on the thick walls contributes as much to the drama of the interior as do the juxtapositions of brilliant Mexican colors. Mr. Barragan designed most of the furniture, which is austere but contemporary in the Mexican idiom.

1. In the rooftop terrace, planes of color are composed like a surrealistic painting, made all the more arresting by the changes of alternating light and shadow, moving clouds, and sky.

2. The work area is dominated by Mr. Barragan's famous floating, natural-pine stairs. Furnishings are low and unpretentious, accentuating the grandeur of the room and the high ceilings. A double thickness of curtains shades the room from the brutal Mexican sun.

3. Partitions divide the living room into three separate areas; work, library, sitting. The mood of each area is different, offering an interesting variety; but there is an aesthetic consistency to the whole.

4. The formally arranged sitting area looks out on a poetically disheveled garden, a de-

lightful contrast in atmosphere and setting. Mr. Barragan displays some of his art on an oversize lectern and along a bookcase, giving the room a wonderfully comfortable, unpretentious feeling. A fireplace is installed in the wall on the right. In order to vary the landscape, cream-colored half-curtains are used on the inside and full-length ones outside. The pine floors are left unpolished.

Photographs by Jon Naar

49

1

2

3

4

Colin St. John Wilson and M. J. Long

The studio that sculptor Sir Reid Dick built in the garden of his London house in 1922 had the kind of charm and space that Colin St. John Wilson and M. J. Long, his wife, found irresistible. They converted the studio into a residence by adding such necessities as a kitchen and an entrance hall and by refurbishing the entire space. Records that Mr. Wilson and Ms. Long found indicated that the studio was designed by a Glasgow architectural firm; judging by the Charles Rennie Mackintosh–like detailing in the columns and balustrading of the main gallery, the architect-in-charge was clearly much influenced by the master's style and sense of proportion.

In the architectural additions Mr. Wilson and Ms. Long have made to the house, they respected the Mackintosh timber-design tradition. His impact can be seen in a storage-and-screen unit they added to the gallery and in a new staircase that leads upstairs from the entrance hall to the bedrooms.

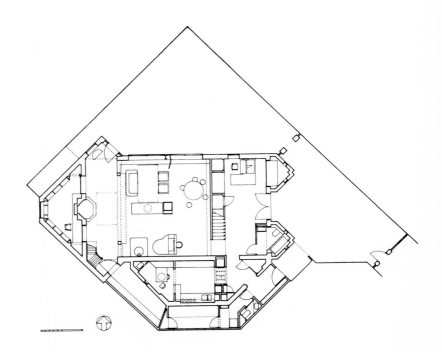

Mr. Wilson and Ms. Long focused attention on the spectacularly large north windows by covering them minimally with matchstick roller blinds and planting them with vines that cascade down raffishly. Lamps hanging from the ceiling emphasize the dramatic volumetric character of the space.

1. The design of the new staircase reflects the style of the columns and balustrading original to the studio. The chair with a black-and-white cushion is a reproduction of a design by Josef Hoffmann. The proportions of the entrance have been made ample enough to accommodate an office.

2. In the attractive kitchen, ivy trails down in front of the windows and along a shelf. A clerestory brings the natural daylight into the kitchen and the utility area beyond. Because of the skylight and excessive ceiling height, the modestly scaled room seems much larger than it is. Quarry-tile floors blend well with the wooden counter tops and the profusion of plants.

3. A bookshelf was built in along the full length of the north windows. A long, low case of drawers and a drinks cart by Alvar Aalto effectively isolate the seating area from the rest of the room.

4. The stove, a survivor from earlier times, though no longer used for heating, still serves aesthetically to scale down the monumental size of the room. A warm-air heating system with grills installed along the windowsill takes its functional place. The large paintings are perfectly sized for the enormous room.

5. Besides being an agreeable get-away-from-it-all haunt, the gallery, with its newly added superstructure, serves as a useful storage area. The free-standing screen in the living room is Egyptian; the rugs, Persian.

1

3

2

4

5

Warren Cox

Perhaps one of the most difficult design tasks is to blend new architectural details harmoniously with old. When renovating an old house of some architectural distinction, melding sometimes seems so forced that architects may prefer to obliterate old detailing altogether and start completely fresh. Taking a different approach, Warren Cox delighted in the original architectural elements in his tall and narrow Victorian house in Georgetown, in Washington, D.C., and chose to absorb them, in both shape and spirit, when putting his own design stamp on the interior. The semicircular fan light over the front door gave him his formal theme. He executed this motif throughout the house in many different variations: a circle cut in the hall—living-room wall, a fan-shaped opening over the library—dining-room door, an arch in the partition between the library and living room.

Mr. Cox used light architecturally in both the living room and the dining room.

In the living room a huge cube of light shines down on a coffee table illuminated from within by incandescent bulbs placed under a frosted glass top. And in the dining room a new ceiling that carries out the curve of the fan-shaped overdoor is washed with light on all sides, making it appear to float.

An avid collector of art and objects—with never enough space for either—Mr. Cox built a picture ledge for prints and drawings around the perimeter of the living room and mounted lights on a track above it. In the dining room he displayed old objects in a series of lighted niches that run like a frieze between the bookshelves and banquettes.

1. French doors on either side of a window that is capped with a fan-shaped curve lead to a terrace. A new curved ceiling, suspended on rods from the old ceiling, provides soft general lighting for the dining room. Serving counters are cantilevered along one wall.

Thonet chairs with cane seats surround the dining table, which Mr. Cox made from a door.

2. A circle in the living-room wall admits an additional supply of daylight from the bright front hall. The mantelpiece was stripped down to its original pine. Beige linen upholstery combines casually with sisal carpets and plants. Early American weather vanes and an antique toy car are perfectly at home with a collection of modern prints.

3. In the bedroom, bookshelves with concealed storage below are built as a strip around the room. A box running along the window wall allows plants optimal daylight. Padded benches with canvas covers are constructed like old-fashioned window seats. The mock fireplace is an assemblage of an arch found in the house, columns from another fireplace, and a white marble fountainhead discovered in Maine.

4. Bookcases are built to the ceiling in the

library, with storage recessed above and underneath. Banquettes are upholstered in lambskin.

Photographs by Robert Lautman

57

1

2

3

Georgie Wolton

A derelict cottage was the only existing building on the eighty acres of farmland in East Hasley, Surrey, England, that Georgie Wolton was given by her mother. She decided to tear down the cottage but kept its spirit very much alive in the compact glass house, called Fieldhouse, she designed to take its place. The sweeping views are splendidly romantic—the Thames Valley to the north and a group of nineteeth-century flint farm buildings to the south. Fieldhouse is not only used as a vacation retreat but also as a headquarters for an afforestation program Ms. Wolton has begun by planting thousands of beech trees.

The house has a steel frame and a heat-absorbent skin of brown-colored glass. To keep the rooms warm in the coldest and dampest weather, the ceiling is radiant heated electrically, and anthracite glows warmly in a stainless steel stove.

The planning of the interior is simplicity itself. In the center is a bath-kitchen core; on one side is the living-dining area and on the other a master bedroom and a child's bedroom. Every room in the house, except the bathroom, partakes of the poetic vistas. Splattered generously over the dark cork floors is Ms. Wolton's remarkable collection of colorful kilim carpets. The furnishings are appropriately casual and low key.

1. To the left as you enter is the master bedroom. Directly in front of the entrance is the bathroom-kitchen core, which divides the house into sleeping and living areas.
2. Along the back of the house, directly opposite the entrance hall, is a child's bedroom, the kitchen, and the dining area. When the sliding doors are recessed into the wall, it is possible to enjoy a sweeping view out both ends and along one side of the house.
3. In the living area banquettes and the dining table offer views of fires in the stove

as well as views of the surrounding landscape. A desk fits unobtrusively into the corner.

Photographs by Richard Einzig, © Brecht-Einzig Ltd.

61

1

2　3

Michel Sadirac

The combination of a neighboring fifteen-floor-high skyscraper, a busy street, and a very small lot made Michel Sadirac decide to build his rectangular concrete-block-and-cement house in Bordeaux, France, to the boundaries of his site. A concrete-block wall surrounds it. No windows penetrate the protective shield of privacy the wall provides. Instead, Mr. Sadirac brings daylight into the house from two gardens (exterior, planned as part of the house, and interior) and two small patios.

The living room is divided into two areas: one is open and airy, particularly ideal for warm weather socializing; the other is a tight conversation arena built around a fireplace. Fabric-covered, floor-to-ceiling sliding panels screen both the master bedroom and the kitchen from the main living area. This arrangement enables the cook to be a part of the general conversation while preparing meals, with the option of closing off any disarray in the kitchen afterward.

The interior garden gets an ample

supply of daylight from a sliding glass element in the ceiling that is shaded from direct sunlight by a deep crosswork of boards painted white.

1. The living area and child's bedroom open onto the garden (as does the master bedroom, not pictured here). A simple built-in unit in the living area was designed by Mr. Sadirac to incorporate bolsters and cushions, as well as tables and bookshelves. In the dining area Thonet chairs surround a white Formica table on a simple chrome base.

2. The fireplace seating pit consists of stone-covered steps softened with cushions and illuminated by a lamp in a large paper shade. A huge concrete hood over the open fireplace is painted black. A bookshelf spans the two walls to the left. The master bedroom is located behind sliding panels.

3. The crosshatching of wood in the ceiling throws interesting patterns of light and shade on the panels dividing the kitchen

from the living area. Both the dining area and the kitchen can participate in the delightful vista of the lush interior garden. The galley kitchen is efficiently arranged with work space and sink on one side; and storage space, oven, refrigerator and washing machine on the other, in tall cabinets that give the wall a pristine, uniform look.

Photographs by Carla de Benedetti

65

1
2

3

William J. Conklin

That simple, beautifully proportioned architectural details of any period blend harmoniously is demonstrated by William J. Conklin in his New York town house, vintage 1862. Cornices, moldings, recesses, and fireplace are ornate (but not floridly so), whereas the Conklin additions of built-in storage, window coverings, and track lighting are austerely functional. But the old and the new not only harmonize with each other, they also bring out the essence of each other by way of contrast.

Mr. Conklin, who in his spare time collects and restores ancient Peruvian textiles, has managed the difficult feat of providing easily accessible storage for all the bits and pieces of his hobby, with none of the usual oppressiveness that comes from clutter and a sensation of being overwhelmed by too much "stuff."

The parlor floor is divided into a study area at one end and a living area at the other. There is no transitional jolt from work to relaxation realms, because built-ins

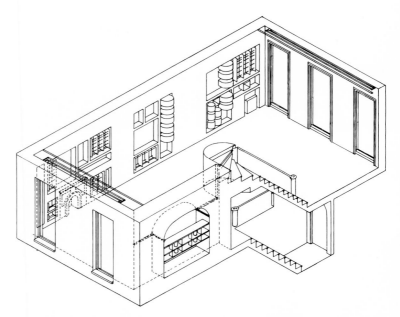

and furnishings throughout the room are stylistically as one. In the study area Mr. Conklin keeps his projectors and photographic slides, containers for multicolored yarns and threads for keeping the textiles in condition, rolled-up drawings, and books. In the living area he displays his textiles and toys on the wall; he accommodates more books, records, and music equipment on built-in shelves.

1. A library stepladder of Mr. Conklin's design moves on ball bearings to give ready access to items stored on high shelves. Transparent plastic cylinders for plans and drawings, half-oval white plastic boxes for graphic and photographic supplies and weaving tools, clear plastic drums for carousels, and wooden boxes for slide projectors, all clip onto metal wall tracks. A standard art-supply cabinet with a carpeted top holds the textiles and makes a handy extra table or bench.

2. Blue plastic sunshades in front of the windows protect the textiles by screening out ultraviolet rays, and also add an interesting color effect. The 1862 alcove was fitted out by Mr. Conklin with shelves for books and music. Lighting in the shelves washes the walls and ceiling.

3. The storage wall continues into the living area with a panoramic display of exotic textiles (most were once ponchos) and antique toys. In order to minimize dust accumulation, books are stored on racks of plastic tubing rather than on solid shelves.

4. White shutters at the windows and greenery soften the crisp outlines of the study area. A white nylon umbrella lamp looks pleasantly whimsical.

Photographs by Norman McGrath

69

Alberto Seassaro

From the ordered, precise look of this apartment, it would be hard to predict that it is a vacation haunt located in an old fisherman's house in Camogli, near Portofino, Italy. But Alberto Seassaro has chosen to define the various spaces and set out the various functions of his apartment with a modular system of lacquered white wood slats. He even utilizes these slats as the primary design component of his furniture. The slats are assembled into elements that serve as shelves, cabinets, closets, drawers, and lighting fixtures. Combined with sausage-shaped pillows covered in orange fabric, they function for seating as well. The living room was designed to be used in many ways: for entertaining and relaxing as well as for dining and working.

1. White grids delimit storage areas, decorate walls, and outline a dropped ceiling above which lighting is recessed. The plastic sculptures are the works of the architect.
2. The blue ceiling and orange lamp seem particularly vivid against the white walls, lacquered white cagelike constructions, and white tile floor. The table doubles for work or dining.
3. The repetition of slats offers the same economy of line found in a very simple sculpture, and a similar sense of balance and serenity. The economic advantage is not unlike that of factory mass production, where the more items produced, the lower the unit cost. The sausage cushions adapt equally well for use in chairs, hassocks, benches, or even daybeds.

Photographs by Carla de Benedetti

Portofino.

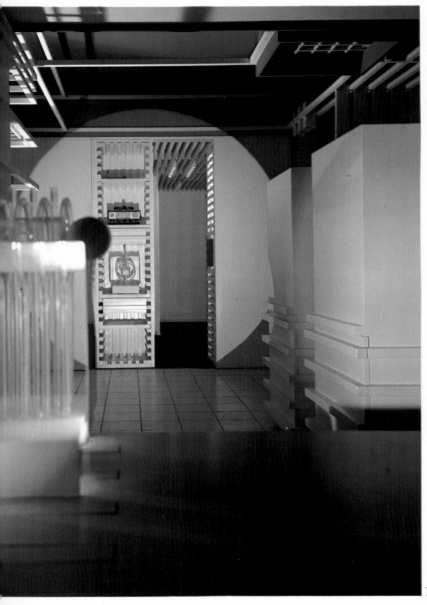

1

2

Nanda Vigo

Before Nanda Vigo let her imagination run wild with the redesign of her apartment in Milan, the space was carved up in a typical late-nineteenth-century manner: a number of small rooms, opening one after another on a central corridor. Ms. Vigo reinterpreted the spirit of the apartment in her own aesthetic terms. An artist who also enjoys collecting, she used gray throughout to provide visual continuity and to focus maximum attention on the art.

She camouflaged a deteriorated old ceiling with a new one of aluminum panels; around the perimeters she installed lighting consisting of coves with neon tubes. The floors throughout are slabs of gray granite; the walls are plaster painted gray. Many of the doors, the storage walls, the window frames, and even some of the furnishings are mirrored.

Ms. Vigo's studio functions as an entrance, an art gallery, and a dining-kitchen area. Furnishings throughout the apartment are a surprising mixture of antiques inherited from Ms. Vigo's grandmother and simple modern pieces, some made to Ms. Vigo's design.

1. The front part of the entrance area is a gallery that displays changing art shows. Pictured here are Ms. Vigo's own works, called light projects. They are of two types, both containing a light source: on the floor are triangles in mirror and steel, on the wall hang glass squares with steel frames. The triangles reflect not only each other but also the simple portable furniture.

2. Also in the entrance area are glass panels, framed in steel, that close off the kitchen area when it is not in use. A cube that doubles as a table and a bar is covered with mirrors.

3. The bathroom was designed as a greenhouse—super luxe. Polished stainless-steel shelves hold different types of plants. The walls are gray marble, edged in the same steel as the shelves.

4. In a guest room Ms. Vigo displays her

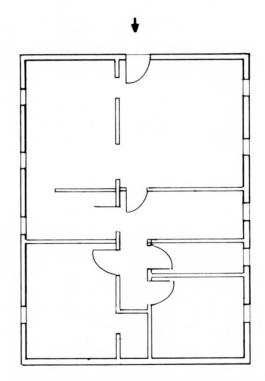

modern-art collection alongside her family antiques. The door and bedside table are mirrored.

5. In Ms. Vigo's bedroom, a stark, mirrored bed is installed in opulent company—an antique mirrored screen, a marble-top table, and a gilded lamp on a black pedestal.

Photographs by Carla de Benedetti

77

1

2

Claudio Dini

To create an enclave of womblike tranquility far above the horn-honking din of Milan, Claudio Dini has blanketed most of his apartment in soothing black—with the exception of a glossy white plaster ceiling, white bookshelves, and white lamps designed by the architect. Besides giving a sense of calm, the black background shows off people, books, plants, and objects to most colorful advantage. Even though the apartment is situated on the top floor of a high-rise apartment building, Dini has managed to make nature an integral part of his interior by converting all the small balconies into oases of plants that flower during the mild weather. Though only token sized, these verdant ledges have the effect of seeming to expand the interior and filling it with a pleasing prospect of light and color.

1. Diners can enjoy a pleasant view of a yellow-awninged balcony green with grass and flowering plants. The serving cabinet of inexpensive chipboard incorporates not only a sink but also burners for warming food and keeping it hot during dinner.

2. Dini's son's room, though small, is chock-a-block with storage space—and with bright color. A white plastic wall is a practical solution to the fingermark problem and is also useful for sticking up prints and posters (and a folding chair that can be taken down for instant extra seating). A lacquered red wall incorporates storage space for out-of season toys and clothes. Ample drawer space is provided in the desk and under the bed. Lighting is hidden behind the wooden laths that form the dropped ceiling.

3. In the living room a conversation area is defined by oversize black velvet-covered cushions brightened by an array of small pillows in bright primary colors. Metal gooseneck lamps form a fascinating snake-like maze over the bookshelf. The stereo equipment and television set are housed in a low storage unit made of the same chipboard used in the dining-room cabinet.

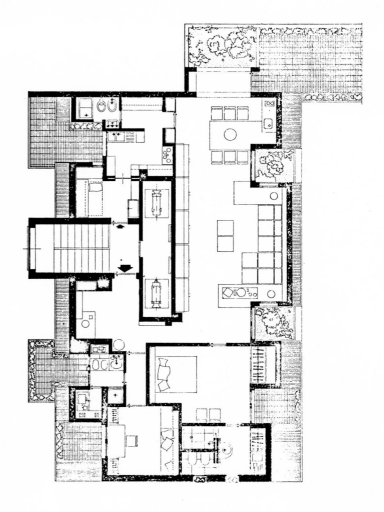

Photographs by Carla de Benedetti   **81**

1

2

3

Harry and Penelope Seidler

Harry and Penelope Seidler took on the challenge of a steep, rocky, "unbuildable" site because they found irresistible the boon of unspoiled, totally protected nature within only eight miles of the center of Sydney, Australia. The sturdy piers on which the house rests and the sweeping balconies and curving roof are a man-made statement as bold as that made by the surrounding rock ledges, towering Eucalyptus trees, rushing stream that turns into a waterfall after a rainstorm, and forever-wild bush preserve. Not a timid, domestic setting this. But every bit a match for the drama of the splendid reinforced concrete house suspended over it.

The house is divided horizontally into four levels. Vertically, a central half-flight of stairs separates the levels into sunny daytime areas and shaded nighttime areas. A free-standing fireplace rises through the central two-and-one-half-story vertical shaft. All the levels open onto terraces that are cool and shaded in the hot summer months.

From the different levels there are glimpses of through views that have none of the predictability of open spaces that lead directly into one another.

Spatial games are played. There are vistas through openings in the fireplace wall, over parapets, around balconies, across the open shaft. The structural materials—concrete, fieldstone, slate flags, brick, wood—have been left in their natural state for subtle contrasts of hues and textures.

1. The efficiently planned galley-like kitchen on the top level of the house is lined with white plastic work surfaces and cupboards. Part of the counter space is set aside as a family eating area. Gray glass sliding doors permit a partial view of the contents of the top cupboards, under which lighting is concealed.

2. The children's playroom, which is on the only level of the house that has direct access to the garden, is positioned so that it can be

seen from both the living room and the dining room. A tapestry by Josef Albers and the brightly colored furniture soften the austerity of the stone wall and floor.

3. In the living room a long oak-framed storage unit with sliding glass panels was planned as a total entertainment center, incorporating television, a bar, sound equipment, and record storage. The unit, which is carefully positioned under the window so as not to interfere with the view, is illuminated from behind by concealed fluorescent strip lighting. The tabletop is of local gray granite.

4. The music room, reached by a short flight of stone steps from the entrance hall, extends the long sweep of the living room. Saarinen pedestal chairs cluster around a Saarinen table. A tapestry by Josef Albers hangs on the wall. The ceiling is lined with oak boards, as it is throughout the house.

5. From the living room it is possible to see beyond the stone fireplace, into the dining

room above and the children's playroom below. The long-haired wool rug and black leather seating pieces contrast effectively with the stone floor and fireplace, and the masonry and concrete walls.

1

2

George D. Hopkins, Jr.

This Victorian cottage, divided down the middle into two "railroad flats," in a style unique to New Orleans, Louisiana, had been abandoned and was in derelict condition when George D. Hopkins, Jr., bought it. He kept all the ornate Victorian detailing of the façade, including the two front doors, and painted the exterior a soft yellow with white trim. He removed the interior dividing walls, leaving five free-standing fireplaces that open on both sides down the center of the house to support the newly exposed ceiling beams.

Natural light floods into the house from four skylights and a gable window, as well as from windows and doors that are left curtainless and shadeless (interior and exterior shrubbery provides needed privacy). At night a hundred bare bulbs mounted between the beams illuminate the house. A large open living room with two fireplaces is located at one end of the house, with an identical family room at the other. Across the middle of the house, a dining room—kitchen area with a central fireplace sep-arates the living room from the family room. Above the dining area, and reached by a ladder, is a loft that affords a spectacular view of the downstairs. Bedrooms are located behind the main house and across a connecting slate patio, in a separate building.

1. The family room makes a pleasant place to lunch on a sunny day. Doors lead out to the bedrooms in the separate building behind the main house.
2. The loft space over the center kitchen-dining area overlooks both the living room and the family room. The chimney for the fireplace in the center of the kitchen-dining area extends through the middle of the loft. Storage areas are located in three of the walls.
3. An oversize Parsons table in the center of the kitchen serves as a breakfast table or an extra work surface. Narrow shelves for spices and packaged foods are attached to the doors of the cleanup center which contains the sink, disposal, and dishwasher.

When the doors are closed, kitchen clutter disappears from view.

4. Light from the skylights and the gable window filters through the crossing beams and reflects on all the walls of the living room. The elimination of frames on windows and doors adds to the clean, crisp feeling of the interior. The symmetrical cube furniture was designed by Mr. Hopkins.

5. There is an uninterrupted flow of space from the living room, through the central dining room—kitchen and on into the family room. The paintings are by Corinne Hopkins.

6. In addition to its soaring spaces and tremendous size, the living room is endowed with two working fireplaces that are open on both sides. White walls, highly polished floors, Oriental rugs, and plants are congenial to the light and airy look of the house. Old-fashioned wingback chairs were brought up to date with a coat of white paint and bright yellow velvet upholstery.

Photographs by George D. Hopkins, Jr.

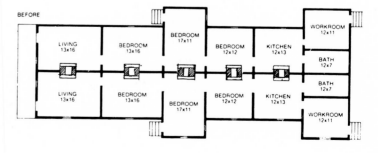

89

1

2

3

4

5

6

Tim Prentice

Many people—particularly apartment or small-house dwellers—dream of the profligacy of space to waste, space to luxuriate in and not have to account for. In usurping all the original part of a Connecticut farmhouse, built in Cornwall in 1790, for a living area and sleeping balcony, Tim Prentice indulged in just such a satisfyingly hedonistic exercise. Originally the room had a seven-foot-high ceiling running through it, but Mr. Prentice ripped that out, displaying in the process the dramatic ceiling line, with its twenty-six-foot-high peak, and the simple purity of the old post-and-beam construction.

At one end of the room Mr. Prentice installed a "people box" with sitting space in the downstairs level and a sleeping space above. From the tight, low-ceilinged sitting area, it is particularly pleasant to gaze into the high, open part of the room with its exposed old beams. Industrial lighting fixtures mounted along the peak of the ceiling in alternating directions temper the lofty scale of the room and wash the walls with light. A stair, cantilevered out six inches beyond its supporting wall, rises jaggedly at the far end of the room like a modern sculpture.

All the new architectural elements in the house are painted with bright orange enamel to set them apart from those of the original structure, which are painted white. The furnishings, mostly simple family hand-me-downs, combine easily with modern Italian chairs and lamps and exotically patterned Indian rugs and textiles.

1. An orange enamel frame encloses the "people box." The seating, covered with Indian throws, was built in at right angles to and opposite the old cooking fireplace, which Mr. Prentice uncovered. Bookshelves fill the space between the windows. Small Luxo lamps are attached to the window frames for reading at night in the cozy, cave-like area. The striped rug is Indian. One of the oldest sunlamps ever made decorates the mantel.

2. Stairs in the high-ceiled part of the living room lead to a guest sleeping area. An old phonograph horn and a dress form add nostalgic, sculptural touches. The orange rug is tie-dyed.

Photographs by Norman McGrath

1

2

Charles W. Moore

An 1894 complex of factory buildings, complete with a waterfall and a mill pond, lured Charles W. Moore to move from New Haven (where he had been Chairman of the Yale School of Architecture) to Essex, Connecticut. The way the buildings were set was ideal for Mr. Moore because he could install his office in an old brick factory building and take over an adjoining tool shed, together with a small wood-frame building, for his home.

He removed the ceiling of the tool shed, and in the two-story space installed a kitchen, bathroom, and stairway, with a bridge across to the second floor of the adjacent Victorian building. He painted the entire structure in red, white, and blue stars and stripes to match the pattern of a napkin he found in a restaurant.

The second floor, which formerly had been a high-ceilinged union hall, Mr. Moore converted into his bedroom–living room. (The downstairs, not shown, is used as a study and a place to house Mr. Moore's collection of thirty thousand color slides.) A twelve-foot-high pyramid in the center of the room delimits separate functions for the free-flowing space without cutting it up or closing it off. One side of the pyramid has been carved out into niches and platforms to display Mr. Moore's collection of electric trains, lead soldiers, and other toys. The other side contains a dressing area with a dresser and closets, and has a wall with hollowed-out niches that serves as a headboard for Mr. Moore's bed. The mysterious pyramid image on the United States one-dollar bill inspired Mr. Moore to paint his pyramid green and emblazon on the ceiling above it the accompanying mottoes *Annuit Coeptis* and *Novus Ordo Seclorum*. Once Mr. Moore had the pyramid painted green, it reminded him of a watermelon as well, so he added pink insides and a white rind.

A storage closet at the end of the room, and overlooking the pond and waterfall, was opened up into a large bay window with built-in seating. The wooden floors, walls, and ceilings were all refinished. Mr. Moore furnished the house eclectically, mostly with antiques and hand-built pieces of furniture, and filled it generously with his collections of knickknacks, paintings, and drawings.

1. By containing all clutter within the solid geometry of the pyramid, the impact of the space, which sweeps up along the roof lines, is intensified. Color has been used with temerity—in the boxy built-in seating units, in cushions covered with bright Marimekko fabrics, in the pipes, and in the pyramid. White paint at the window end of the room relieves the heaviness of the dark wood.

2. One side of the pyramid is carved out to hold closets and an old chest painted bright purple. A Marimekko spread on the bed inspired the flamboyant color scheme.

3. In the former tool shed a small dining area has been installed next to the kitchen and under the protective canopy of the bridge leading to the second-floor living quarters. The blue of the bridge is echoed

in the storage shelves and cut-pile carpeting on the floor.

4. A seating bay has been ensconced in the space previously occupied by a storage closet. The mattresses, single-bed size and covered in Marimekko cotton, provide comfortable lounging and extra sleeping space.

Photographs by Robert Perron

97

1

2

3

Luigi Capriolo and Jacek Popek

This one-room apartment in Milan has been totally furnished with one piece of furniture. Architect Luigi Capriolo, in collaboration with Jacek Popek, has not used magic to conjure up one island of furniture to fulfill all his sleeping, working, entertaining, and dining needs. Instead, he has very carefully designed a system whereby table, bed, desk, and extra seating all fold away neatly or pull out at a moment's notice. The navy blue walls, carpet, and ceiling create a giant tent supported by two shiny white props that coincide with the points where the lamps are placed. Sky-blue arches on the walls echo and reinforce the effect of those in the deeper blue.

1. In the living-room arrangement the furniture island gorges forth a banquette padded with a host of pillows encased in various prints, and a desk with a matching seat.

2. For the dining-room a white plastic-laminated table emerges, flanked by three seats that slide into slots on either side of the lacquered blue platform.

3. A small entrance hall gives a preview of the room's color scheme: light blue on dark blue ballooning arches, with accents of white and shiny red trim.

4. The bed, covered with a black-and-white fake-fur fabric, springs forth complete with night tables and a bar for maintaining a nightcap at arm's reach.

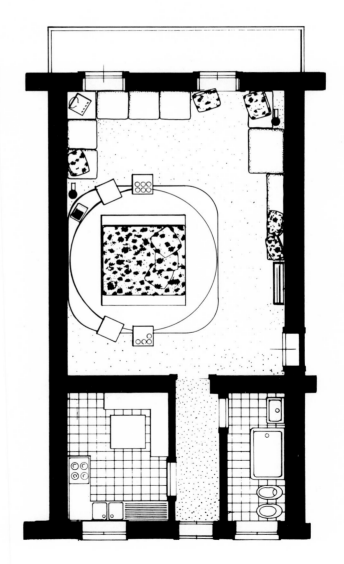

Photographs by Carla de Benedetti

1

2

3

4

Hanford Yang

A superabundance of space, which is the great advantage of living in a loft, can seem so desirable that it often offsets the disadvantages of a run-down condition. So it was for Hanford Yang, who acquired 2500 square feet of loft space in New York City's SoHo area—along with rusted plumbing, uneven floors, and a falling tin ceiling. What mattered most to Mr. Yang was the amount of raw space, thirty-five feet by eighty feet of it, which he secured as a background for the display of his spectacular art collection.

He nestled the bedroom, kitchen, dining area, and bathroom into one corner of the loft and gave all the rest of it to a living room—gallery. Thanks to thirteen-foot-high ceilings, Mr. Yang was able to divide his loft into levels that not only make art viewing more of an exciting, fluid experience but also define functions such as sitting, eating, and sleeping. He left the center of the living area open, except for the row of original cast-iron columns, and placed a seating unit on one side of the space and a long storage cabinet on the other. The entire loft is carpeted in gray, with white walls and natural wood surfaces, to focus attention on the art, which includes works by such contemporary artists as Louise Nevelson, Frank Stella, and Morris Louis, as well as glass by Tiffany and a window by Frank Lloyd Wright. Even with the vastness of his space, Mr. Yang has room to display only one tenth of his collection at any given time, so he changes the entire display of artwork yearly.

Mr. Yang's lovely mid-nineteenth-century cast-iron building has become a tourist attraction for two reasons: first, it has been given official landmark status, and second, the blank brick-faced side of the building has been painted by artist Richard Haas with a witty trompe l'oeil showing rows of dummy windows—including one with a cat sitting on the sill.

1. Lights on ceiling tracks illuminate the rich variety of paintings, sculptures, and objects in Mr. Yang's loft. The sitting area,

which is on a raised platform, is enclosed by an abbreviated hexagonal wall covered in gray carpeting. A window by Frank Lloyd Wright hangs nearby.

2. A beautiful collection of Tiffany glass is displayed in the dining area. The minimal furnishings consist of a natural wood table with a high gloss finish and stools by Alvar Aalto.

3. In the bedroom the only eruption of bright color is in the red spread. Both the built-in bed and a triangular night table are carpeted. The chair is by Alvar Aalto.

4. Mr. Yang designed the built-in sitting area, which is softened with black velvet cushions and navy blue pillows. The long storage unit holds stereo equipment, books, and records.

Photographs by Norman McGrath

1

2

3

4

Barton Choy

Barton Choy set himself the challenge of building the best three-bedroom house he could on the tightest possible budget. He chose a lot 50 by 150 feet in central Los Angeles, California, that was relatively inexpensive because it was both steep and narrow. Although Mr. Choy would have preferred to locate his house at the top of the lot to take advantage of the best views, the height and distance from the street would have made the cost of transporting materials prohibitive. However, he was able to satisfy his desire for a view by a compromise; he mounted the house atop the street-level garage and installed in front a bronzed glass window wall that thrusts outward like a great triangular prow. He pared expenses further by keeping detailing and materials simple—natural red-cedar siding on the exterior and wallboard throughout the interior —and limited the square footage to only 1720 square feet in all.

1. A bright red L-shaped wall screens the

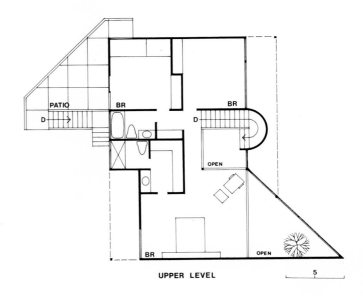

UPPER LEVEL

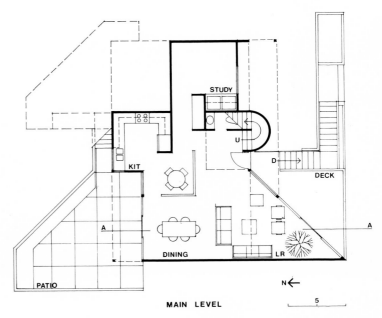

MAIN LEVEL

kitchen from the living area. A view of the hills can be enjoyed from the windows over the sink. Birch cabinets and white Formica counter tops complement one another crisply.

2. The upper half of the tall living-room window provides the master bedroom with natural light and a view of the treetops. A high railing gives privacy. A counterpoint to the sleek, controlled graphics is a wild-looking Chinese ceremonial lion.

3. The street number is hewn from the same natural red cedar as the exterior siding.

4. Mr. Choy painted a colorful bull's eye on two walls to add visual excitement to his son's sparsely windowed room. A patio cut into the hillside compensates for the lack of glass here. Carpeting, the same throughout the house, is an inexpensive commercial grade laid over plywood.

5. Brightly colored banners hanging above the railing of the balcony call immediate attention to the dramatic upward sweep of the living room. Both the sitting area and the

dining area are protectively positioned under the low-ceilinged balcony for added coziness. From the dining area sliding glass doors lead onto a patio. Bare bulbs controlled by a dimmer switch provide inexpensive lighting for the dining area.

Photographs by Glen Allison   **109**

1

2

3

4

Romano Juvara

The large living room of a house in the center of Milan has been inventively renovated by Romano Juvara with a radical, strong interior design. Its effectiveness depends first and foremost on a daring use of color and second on a repetition of modular forms. The few pieces of furniture in the room—a bar-tower incorporating a television set, a study-tower surrounded by a writing desk top, a long table, and a bookcase—are based on a common geometry. They are all parallelepipeds, colored from blue to green to red and intersected by yellow bars. As an almost-matched group they combine to create an unusual play of color and space.

1. The shiny red dining table, bisected by a dark blue stripe that continues down to the floor as a supporting member, is a lively setting for dishes of any color but particularly the chrome yellow ones shown.
2. In a side view the three supporting pedestals for the table can be seen as echoing the cube form of the bar. When the bar is not in use, the front panel is pulled shut to keep bottles and glasses out of sight.
3. The desk top angles around to accommodate two people working at the same time. The lights are recessed inside the parallelepiped.
4. A free-standing black leather sofa, though modern, looks surprisingly sedate in contrast to the unconventionally designed battery of brightly colored shelves, tables, and storage boxes.

Photographs by Carla de Benedetti

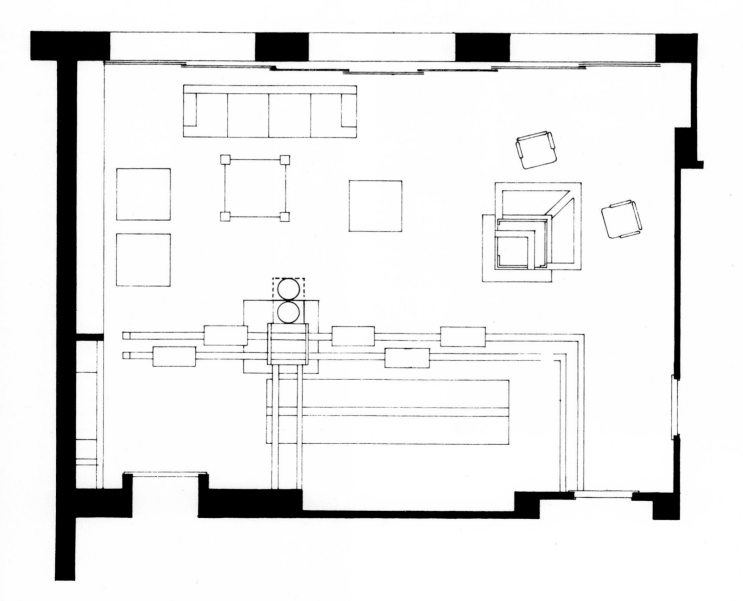

1

2

3

4

Gae Aulenti

Because most people who live in apartments are cursed with relatively low ceilings, they have to content themselves with living "horizontally" in boxlike spaces. Not Gae Aulenti. Her apartment in Milan is located on two floors over her studio. The Aulenti complex fills a narrow four-story building and has a roof terrace on top. Rather than carving the raw space up into cubicles, Ms. Aulenti lets it flow—up, down, and across levels connected by a red metal staircase, a small red metal bridge, and a white walkway. The different zones are defined, for the most part, not by walls, but by low bookcase units that do not impede the exhilarating fluidity of light and space.

It is Ms. Aulenti's belief that the activities she enjoys most—listening to music, talking to friends, enjoying objects, art, and books—should spill over from area to area. Thus there are only three doors in the entire apartment: one at the entrance, another on the kitchen to prevent cooking odors from escaping into the living area, and a third on the bedroom.

From almost anywhere in the apartment it is possible to look beyond and see other areas, with their intriguing varieties of shapes, colors, and textures. The walkways and bridges lend a playful excitement that adds to the joy of living there.

1. The kitchen is divided from the dining area by a wall that contains cubicles for a laundry, a pantry, and a toilet. Wine, cookbooks, condiments in jars, and prints on the walls add color and interest to the all-white arrangement of counters, cabinets, and machines. A simple wooden table provides an extra work surface.

2. A small entrance room, a transition space between the studio and the apartment, is used as a study. Ms. Aulenti designed the steel-and-glass table. A nineteenth-century patchwork quilt from Connecticut hangs on the wall.

3. A walkway, reached by red metal stairs from the living area below, leads to a narrow red metal bridge that gives access to a small veranda, used for listening to music, and the roof terrace beyond. Behind the bookshelves are the master bedroom, a dressing room, and a bath. The low storage unit that separates the living and dining areas holds books on one side and displays paintings by Ceroli, Pistoletto, and Schiffano on the other. A large mask at the end of the walkway is Chinese; the hanging cylinder is Indian.

4. In the living area, bookcases set at right angles screen off the dining area. The sofa, which resembles a double bed, is covered in canvas. The bridge over the sofa leads to the veranda-terrace.

5. A red metal staircase leads from the living area to the walkway. Under the stair is a fifteenth-century sculpture and an enormous vase decorated with polychrome designs. Hanging on the wall in the background is a tapestry by Roy Lichtenstein.

Photographs by Carla de Benedetti

117

1

2

3

4

5

Robert Sobel

This small but elegant one-story house turns its back on its suburban Houston, Texas, surroundings to look inward at a lovely private garden atrium. Robert Sobel designed all the rooms to have access to this central garden through floor-to-ceiling glass walls and doors. Inside the glass, panels made like folding doors control the amount of light and shade and, when closed, provide privacy and security. Skylights throughout the house produce a fascinating play of light and shadow on the natural brick floors. A lavish arraying of plants within the house provides a pleasing counterpoint to the greenery in the atrium. The colors of the interior are kept subdued to give full drama to the abundant plant life.

Even though the house is compact, it accommodates up to two hundred people at one time for parties because the space circulates in a continuous flow around the central garden.

1. In the kitchen a desk, strategically lo-

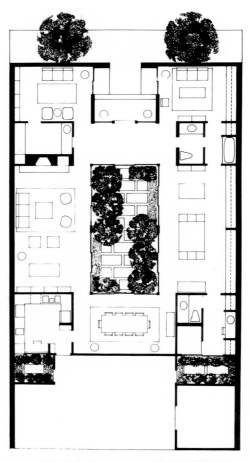

cated for studying cookbooks, writing out menus, or paying bills, overlooks a small extra garden area at the far end of the house. The butcher-block desk top is also utilized as an extra work surface in the kitchen when elaborate cooking is underway.

2. The bed was designed by Mr. Sobel to double as extra seating at parties. The head-board and footboard can serve as tables on those occasions. The work table functions as an extra dining table at large gatherings.

3. In the quietly classic living room, Charles Eames leather lounge chairs and ottomans and a simple black leather sofa are grouped around a coffee table designed by Mr. Sobel. A platform in front of the fire-place provides extra seating.

Photographs by Rick Gardner

1

2   3

William Morgan

A giant sand dune suggested the shape for William Morgan's oceanside house in Atlantic Beach, Florida. The four levels of the house terrace down the dune to the beach, which, along with the ocean, serves as the front yard. In form, the house is two triangles butted against each other. A border of glass around the larger triangle on the side where it meets the smaller one floods the main living space with daylight. The house is completely open on the ocean façade but blank toward the street façade and on the two sides, to screen it from neighboring houses. Concrete foundations and pilings are strong enough to stand up to the worst storms.

Mr. Morgan left the lowest, or beach, level without electrical outlets, in case the sea should inundate it. This area is used for Ping-Pong and the storage of boats and beach paraphernalia. The next level contains the boys' bedrooms, each with a private recessed deck and a bath and work area. The third level on the beach side (which corresponds to the entrance level on the street side) encompasses a thirty-foot-high, central living-dining-kitchen space with a peaked ceiling. Overhanging it and comprising the top level is a balcony incorporating the master bedroom and office.

Mr. Morgan adapted his plan from the ancient Roman city of Herculaneum, a seaside community on the Mediterranean that thrived at the time of Pompeii. At its lowest level Herculaneum had public baths and a beach-oriented area. Above that was an area for changing clothes, and over that a level for dining. On the top or fourth level private residences or apartments were located.

Since nothing is drearier than the seaside on a bleak day, Mr. Morgan chose terra-cotta carpeting and light woods—natural cedar walls and white-pine ceilings—to make the interior of the house seem sunny and bright, even when it wasn't.

1. The night view of the house, with the interior lighting shining out through the many glass openings, is particularly spectacular on the two levels of double balconies

124

and in the border of glass where the triangles meet. The kitchen is so close to the beach that food and drink can be brought directly outdoors from the refrigerator.

2. In the master bedroom—office balcony a bookshelf acts as a buffer affording privacy from the two-level living space on the other side. The cedar siding is laid in a pattern of opposing diagonals for added visual interest.

3. A bunk room, one of an identical pair designed for the two Morgan boys, has the same efficiency and economy of space as a ship's cabin. Bookshelves, bunks, and a work table are built in, with the surface left natural like the walls.

4. The kitchen, nestled under the overhang of the balcony where lighting is recessed, is finished in the same light wood as the rest of the open living space to blend unobtrusively with its surroundings.

5. In the major living space, which soars to a height of thirty feet, the overhang of the balcony creates a sheltered and cozy sitting area around the fireplace. The aluminum-based chairs and table were designed by Mr.

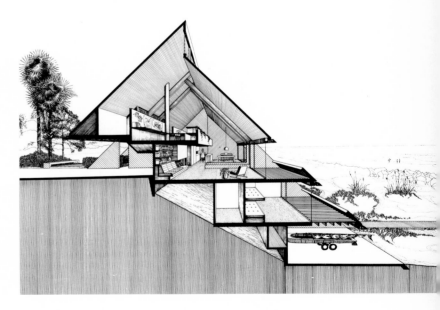

Morgan, as was the wooden lighting cube over the dining table.

Photographs by W. Newton Morgan, Jr.

1

2

3

4

5

Hugh Newell Jacobson

When remodeling a house in the historic district of Georgetown, in Washington, D.C., Hugh Newell Jacobson did not have the architect's usual artistic license to create exactly what he pleased. Instead, he had to work within the aesthetic discipline of the conservative, old-fashioned architectural look of the neighborhood. Mr. Jacobson renovated the original 1840 Federal-style house to accommodate a dining room on the first floor and one bedroom each on the second and third floors, and built a two-story addition to house two more bedrooms and all the major living areas. By placing the visible parts of the addition behind the existing garden wall and moving the main entrance to the garden side, off what is now an entry courtyard, and removing the old portico, he has blended the house into the neighborhood without sacrificing the abundance of new glass he wanted for a sense of light and openness.

An original bay, located in the dining room in the front of the house, is matched by a new bay at the opposite end of the house in the newly added living room. From the old bay it is possible to look the length of the house, through floor-to-ceiling sliding glass pocket doors to a terrace-garden.

The house is ideal for entertaining large groups because all the rooms on the first floor have at least two doors, allowing an easy circulation. The living room and the library, which adjoin each other, both give onto a terrace paved with bluestone, and a garden planted with dogwood trees, holly, and English ivy and brightened by tubs and pots of colorful flowers. The garden walls, approximately ten feet high, reflect soft natural light into both the living room and library.

1. Daylight is introduced into the kitchen through a skylight above a four-by-ten-foot well that extends up through the master bathroom on the second floor. The efficiently

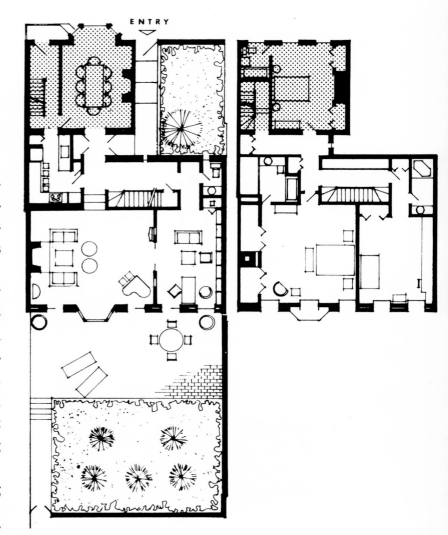

planned area is all white, with bright terra-cotta quarry-tile floors. A work area illuminated by the light well doubles as a break-fast counter, with four Thonet stools underneath for seating.

2. In the dining room, which was originally the living room, the old windows were replaced with floor-to-ceiling sash windows. A fifteenth-century French refectory table repeats the dark tones of the stained oak floors. Shutters at the windows, a fern in an old brass plant stand, and Thonet chairs contrast effectively with the modern lineal painting by Gene Davis.

3. The library opens to the adjoining living room as well as to the terrace-garden. Mr. Jacobson designed the love seat made of white oak strip flooring. The desk, optimally placed to receive lavish quantities of daylight, can accommodate two.

4. The yellow-and-white color scheme of the living room derives from a painting by Josef Albers. Mr. Jacobson designed the Fiberglas and plywood sofas. Floor-to-ceiling doors, opening to the terrace-garden, make the room seem larger than its actual size.

Photographs by Robert Lautman

129

1

2

3

Ulrich Franzen

The rush and din of New York City seems far away from the natural light, peace, and comfort of Ulrich Franzen's rooftop aerie. Mr. Franzen chose as the hub for his penthouse apartment a fluid space, fifty feet by thirty-five feet, in which he created a living area, a dining area, and a study. The divisions are made not by floor-to-ceiling walls that cut down on precious light and space, but by fin walls, low partitions, or changes in floor level. Because of the subtlety of the screening, one is not overwhelmed by the vastness of the space but rather intrigued by changing vistas from one space to another.

One of the great joys of penthouse living, besides the spectacular views, is the rare center-city opportunity to bask in splendid natural light. Here the study, the living area, and the master bedroom run the length of a north terrace that floods the apartment in north light. A large sky dome placed over the interior dining area adds a plentiful dose of south light.

For nighttime use Mr. Franzen installed artificial lighting that creates equally dramatic, but entirely different, effects. Wall and floor lights wash the interior in reflected light. A fluorescent cove built into the windowsill, inches above the floor of the living space, acts as a light bridge between indoors and out, where the terrace and its planting are illuminated.

A greenhouse on the north side of the apartment was converted into a study with the addition of an electric heating element to take off wintry chills, and an air-conditioning unit for summer. (The first owner of the apartment, James J. Walker, New York City's prohibition mayor, had the greenhouse built as a special present for Marian Corbet when she lived here.)

1. The bedroom overlooks the north terrace and benefits from its bounty of natural light. Mr. Franzen designed the bed and headboard to fit into the protective angle of the

walls. The tractor-seat chairs are also a Franzen design.

2. The bathroom, with its wide expanse of mirror and built-in lighting, is designed to double as a dressing room. Brown and silver Mylar wallpaper makes the small space seem larger than it is.

3. A large domed skylight provides the dining area with natural light, even though it is far removed from any windows. The white oak dining table is a Franzen design. The sculpture is by Louise Nevelson. Beyond, the library can be seen.

4. The library is a cozy, comfortable retreat with a wall covered with books and objects. There are two Charles Eames lounge chairs. Mr. Franzen designed the coffee table and the reading lamp.

5. The study, formerly a greenhouse, overlooks the large penthouse terrace on the west side.

6. The large central space of the penthouse is divided by half walls and level changes

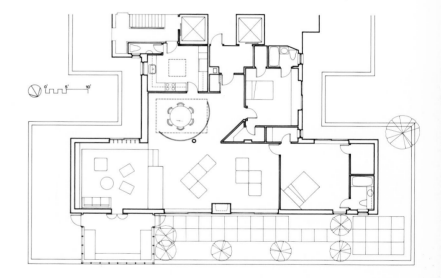

into a library, a dining area (behind the orange half-wall), and a living area. Mr. Franzen encased the round column in mirror-finish stainless steel in honor of Mies van der Rohe. The coffee-colored couches by Mario Bellini seem to grow out of the coffee-colored rug.

Photographs by David Franzen and Norman McGrath

133

1

2

3

4

5

6

Ziona Leshem

Having had to spend more of her budget than she had anticipated on the site she especially desired—a small piece of land right on the Mediterranean in Heraliya, Israel—Ziona Leshem needed to design a house for her family with the maximum space at the least cost. As a method of construction she chose a cast-concrete process invented by Haim Heiftz, in which three domes, each appropriately thirty-three feet in diameter and sixteen feet high, were made by pouring concrete over a balloon of canvas and rubber that was inflated by an electrical engine. After the concrete had set for three days, the balloon was deflated and reused for the next dome. A network of iron in the concrete helps to stabilize and strengthen the shell.

The first dome, with an opening approximately sixteen feet in diameter cut into the top, forms a patio—abloom with exotic plants—through which one passes before entering the house. A transition space between the street and the house, the patio offers total privacy from the street. The second dome contains a foyer, a two-story-high living room with views to the sea, and a kitchen, which sits in the space like a great piece of round sculpture. The third dome is divided into two stories, with bedrooms and bathrooms both on the first floor and Ms. Leshem's studio, reached by a narrow spiral staircase, on the second.

Concrete walls, inside and out, are left rough cast and natural. The round windows were made simply, with the glass fixed straight into the concrete. During the summer, awnings shade the windows from the bright sun. The furniture was collected on travels all over the world: antiques from Europe, old chests from Taiwan, and Persian rugs.

1. A concrete seat, cast as part of the foyer, overlooks the living room below and the sea beyond. Floor mosaics, approximately three feet in diameter and ringed with brass strips, start in the foyer and continue into the liv-

136

ing room. The kitchen looks like a rough concrete promontory rising out of the living room. In the latter, a water bed covered with a flokaty rug, and low enough not to interfere with the view, is another choice spot for sea watching.

2. From the dining table it is possible to view the patio through a near window and the sea through a window across the room. The brass chandelier hanging over the table is Russian. A short flight of stairs leads up to the foyer; the spiral staircase goes to Ms. Leshem's study.

3. The rounded kitchen is separated from the living room by oak cabinets; a backsplash between the upper and lower cabinets is red Italian ceramic. The counters and the table have identical brown marble tops.

4. Ms. Leshem's studio, a quiet aerie in the top of the third dome, overlooks all the living spaces.

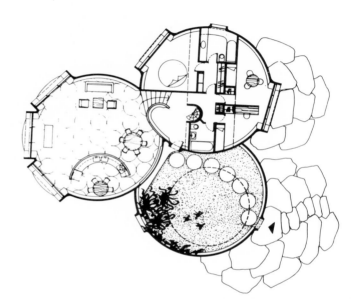

Photographs by Wulf Brackrock

1
2

Anne and Tony Woolner

Philip Johnson's, the most famous of all the transparent houses built in the late 1940s of steel and glass, reflected Bauhaus traditions. Anne and Tony Woolner's 1970s version expresses the space-age aesthetic. And even though logic tells us that the Woolners' streamlined, aerodynamic dwelling in New Salem, New York, will never "lift off," science-fiction fantasizing makes us half wish it could rocket above its rural setting of meadows, corn fields, and rolling hills.

In order to create their 3500-square-foot futuristic-looking house, which is spanking white outside and in, the Woolners adopted some building techniques not often found in residential architecture. They chose for the structural skeleton laminated wood arches usually found as supports for gymnasium ceilings. They borrowed the idea for their window panes—heat-formed, seven-foot plastic squares—from aircraft. The silicone sealing that keeps the forty windows watertight came from space technology.

The Woolners organized their house into an open-to-view public zone, located in a thirty-five-foot-long arched cylinder with twenty-foot-high ceilings, and a private zone consisting of a row of mostly windowless cubes sandwiched between blank-walled silos on either end. The public zone contains the living-dining areas, which flow into each other, and a balcony-studio suspended over the kitchen and workroom. The private zone contains bedrooms, baths, a utility room, and a darkroom.

One of the most appealing aspects of a transparent house is the opportunity it gives for living almost as close to nature as camping under the stars. Rain showers and snowstorms become special experiences. And the fluctuations of natural light provide a continuous spectacle, as the sun and moon cast shifting patterns of light and shadow on the walls and floors. Even on cloudy days it is possible to live quite comfortably without turning on electric lights.

Two five-ton air-conditioning units and some removable opaque panels enable the Woolners to keep cool even in the heat of summer.

1. From the studio, which overhangs the kitchen and workroom, there is a splendid view upward of the sky and clouds and, out the end window wall, of the trees and hills. The bright red upholstery is particularly striking with white walls and white asbestos-tile floors.

2. The master bedroom, located in the private zone, seems almost cavelike when compared with the living area and its ten plastic-covered bays. Windows begin at chin height to assure privacy and slant to a forty-five degree angle for optimum view watching.

3. One large modular seating unit floats as an island for relaxation and entertaining in the sea of white. Stairs lead up to the master bedroom. At night artificial illumination is provided by spotlamps distributed on tracks running along either side of the living area.

4. A divider wall separating the living area from the kitchen and studio-balcony rises only as high as the second row of windows, allowing an uninterrupted flow of space from one end of the cylinder to the other. The furniture is placed in squared-off groupings as a counterpoint to the thrust and movement of the arches. Colors were chosen to echo the surrounding landscape.

Photographs by Anne and Tony Woolner and Louis Reens

141

2

1

3

Christopher H. L. Owen

The problems of building on an island are unique. So are the rewards. The frustrations Christopher H. L. Owen encountered in constructing his vacation house on Block Island, Rhode Island, were primarily economic. His per-square-foot building costs were higher than average because all materials, the contractor, and the work crew were brought from the mainland. But the aesthetic advantages of a rolling meadowland site fringed with bayberry and a spectacular view of the harbor with its passing parade of sailboats more than compensated.

To keep the size of the house down to 1500 square feet, while at the same time taking advantage of the splendid views, Mr. Owen used generous expanses of glass. He shaded the glass from the sun with towers wrapped in vertical red cedar siding, left to weather to a warm gray. One tower contains the stairwell that connects all three levels of the house; the other is open, to provide a tiny sun deck on the first floor. Below is a

utility room and above a sitting area adjoining the master bedroom.

The house is entered by an outside staircase on the southwest side, which is for the most part left blank to shield the house from future development on neighboring sites, and as a screen against the intense summer sun. The main level contains a sixteen-foot-high, two-story living area and a one-story dining area and kitchen. Visual access to the sea is everywhere, even in the master bedroom, where shutterlike doors overlook the living area and the landscape beyond the glass. Three other bedrooms—all bunkrooms with porthole windows—one on the ground floor and two on the top with skylights, are small and efficient.

Sylvia Owen, an interior designer, chose white walls and mostly neutral fabrics to focus attention on the surrounding natural beauty.

1. The master bedroom, located in one of

the towers, just above the deck, has a tiny sitting area next to a window at its far end. Folding shutter doors are left open as much as possible to bring the view into the room and prevent the tight space from seeming claustrophobic. Bright yellow bedspreads and Indian pillows contrast with white walls.
2. The kitchen, with its view of the wild and beautiful moors, is a continuation of the dining area. Its efficient working arrangement features butcher-block counters and overhead cabinets. The floor is covered with soft, low-maintenance Italian rubber flooring.
3. All three bunkrooms are built very much on the principle of a ship's cabins. The nautical feeling is reinforced by porthole windows. There is hanging space behind the door and drawers under the beds for storage.
4. Living and dining areas that flow into each other take mutual advantage of scenic views by day and a fire in the fireplace by night. The furnishings have been kept appropriately understated: in the living room

Breuer chairs covered in white canvas edge a white wool rug; the butcher-block dining table is surrounded by Breuer's classic cane chairs.

Photographs by Christopher H. L. Owen   **145**

1

3

2

Norman Jaffe

Rather than try to build a house that called attention to itself as being radically different from the neighboring houses and farm structures of Bridgehampton, New York, Norman Jaffe chose to reinterpret traditional Long Island summer houses in a modern way. He used cedar shingles on the exterior, and the chimneys, pitched roof, and dormers are all there—but one has almost to look twice to recognize them, so different are they in form from the classical prototypes seen in houses built in the 1920s and 1930s.

Inside, Jaffe separated the house into rooms not so much by walls as by stairs leading to four different levels, and by open balconies. From the entry it is possible to look down into Mr. Jaffe's studio or all the way up two stories to the top-level ceiling, forty-two feet above.

Although the furnishings are minimal and spare, the interior seems tremendously warm because of the rough-sawn cedar paneling used throughout. The dining and living areas share one large space, and on a lower level, but flowing from the living room, is a carpeted conversation pit with a view from a dormerlike extension framed in glass. An oversize chimney incorporates a large skylight that brings daylight deep into the interior of the 3500-square-foot house.

1. A skylight floods the breakfast area with sunshine, making it an ideal place to grow plants. The red of the Magistretti chairs surrounding the marble-topped table is repeated in the kitchen cabinets. A sitting area has been built into the kitchen to keep cook and guests within easy talking distance.
2. From the entry a handsome open staircase of natural wood leads down to the studio and up to the living-room level.
3. The abundance of natural light in the living-dining area comes partly from the oversize skylight in the study on the top level. Because the same Magistretti chairs are used for both the dining room and the breakfast room, extra matched seating is at the ready for large dinner parties.

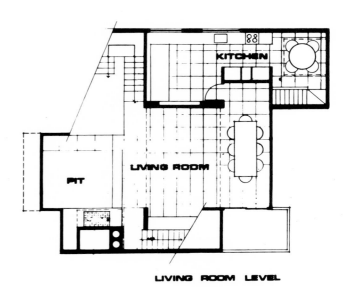

LIVING ROOM LEVEL

4. The guest room on the entry level has its own access to the outdoors through sliding glass doors. A simple built-in bed, closet, walls, and dresser, all of natural wood, focus full attention on the landscape.

5. A dormer window sweeps around one wall of the sunken and carpeted sitting area, while a massive fireplace dominates the other. Broad slate steps lead down from an open living-dining area.

Photographs by Maris / Semel

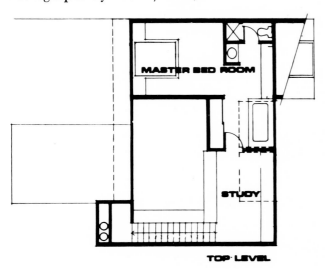

TOP LEVEL

1

2

3

4

5

Peter Chermayeff

"Mother Nature" could have been the client, so sensitively and with such respect did Peter Chermayeff treat her when designing his house near Boston, Massachusetts. Before deciding on a concept, he studied, through four seasons, his peninsular wooded acre of land, jutting into a wildlife refuge pond. During this getting-acquainted phase, Mr. Chermayeff made the decision to design his house in such a way that not one major tree would have to be cut down. He chose an unpretentious form: two two-story cubes, one somewhat larger than the other, joined in the middle by a small cube containing the entrance hall. Windows of various shapes and sizes are cut into the studio façade in locations chosen for framing the best views. A simple wooden deck, raised on concrete pilings seventeen feet above the pond, makes an ideal perch for tree, bird, and wildlife watching. Because Mr. Chermayeff did not wish his house to be so strong a sculptural statement that its silhouette against the landscape would encroach upon the quiet sylvan vistas enjoyed by other neighbors on the pond, he painted the three public sides of the house burnt umber and only the private south side white. The white side acts as a backdrop for the shadowplay of sunlight filtering through the trees.

1. The living room is divided into two parts: an enclosed upper area with two built-in sofas, a fireplace, and a fir ceiling; and a lower area that is so open in feeling it gives the impression of a tree house.

2. A high butcher-block pass-through between the dining area and the kitchen enables cook and guests to communicate while meals are being prepared. A door leads out from the dining area to a walkway that connects the house to the deck over the pond.

3. From the entrance hall, views can be enjoyed through windows above, below, and directly in front. A soft brown carpeting leads the eye gently through the downstairs and out to the woods beyond.

4. A deck, built over the pond on concrete

pilings, is connected to the house by a narrow boardwalk. The railings were carefully designed to blend into the wooded surroundings.

5. The kitchen offers views of the trees and pond through two floor-to-ceiling windows and a glass door opening to the south terrace. Butcher-block tops, oak chairs with rush seats, white walls and cabinets, and quarry-tile floors look crisp and inviting. A square wooden hood over the stove accommodates a collection of spice jars.

Photographs by Peter Chermayeff   153

1

3
4
5

James Lambeth

Change and privacy are the two qualities James Lambeth appreciates most, so it was natural that he would emphasize both in the design of his Fayetteville, Arkansas, house. A golden, mirror-windowed façade reflecting the brilliance of the changing seasons is the dominant feature. When one walks up the fifty-five-foot-long entry bridge to the front door, the windows seem to come alive with leaves—in hues of green or red or gold—or white with snow, depending on the season. Yet because of the golden coating on the mirror glass, the windows screen the interior from outside viewing, while allowing those inside to see out. Thus, though half the house is glass, privacy is assured.

The warmth of cedar siding contrasts pleasantly with the abundance of glass. Both sides of the house are kept windowless to shield it from neighbors and to avoid the east and west sun. The Lambeths use the deck outside the living room as a place for taking sun baths, cooking outdoors, and looking out upon the tree-covered valley to the south.

Because of the steep site, and to expand the vista, the house was raised ten feet off the ground on steel columns.

The furnishings are quietly classic, their neutral colors never at odds with the nature without and the art within.

1. The balcony, reached from the living room by a free-standing winding staircase, doubles as an entrance foyer. Below it, a convenient kitchen–living room pass-through makes for easy entertaining. The parquet flooring was extended up the front of the counter.
2. The living room's two-story window wall brings the outdoors in. The height of the room is emphasized by a tall bamboo tree, the staircase, and a graphic banner of and by Joyce Lambeth.
3. The windows make the guest bathroom a pleasant spot for enjoying the view of the valley and for sunning both people and plants. Blue cabinets and plastic counters complement the burnt-brick exterior-inte-

rior wall. The mobile is by Alexander Calder.

4. The music room on the entrance level of the house is screened from the street by golden-covered mirror glass, which allows Courtney Lambeth to see out but not be observed from the street while she practices the piano. The only color in the calm room comes from the plants and people.

5. The dining room, downstairs on the middle-living-room level, is in one of the two wings and looks out on the entry bridge. A mirrored end wall visually doubles the size of the room and reflects a banner behind the table. The red of the banner is echoed in the plastic chairs. Mr. Lambeth made the wooden table, topping it with black Formica. The lighting fixtures on an overhead track are movable.

Photographs by Larry L. Logan and James Lambeth

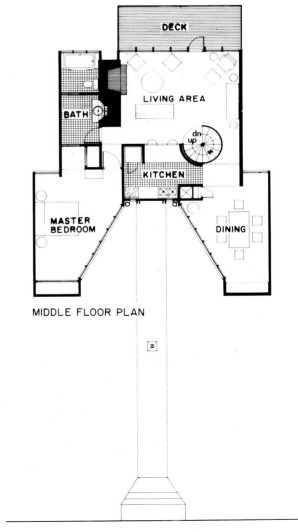

MIDDLE FLOOR PLAN

Vittorio Gregotti

Vittorio Gregotti chose for his home the neo-classic wing of an eighteenth-century palace situated in Piazza Sant'Alessandro, one of the most beautiful squares of the historical center of Milan. Because the four large rooms and huge bathroom contained in the wing were not suitable for a contemporary life, Gregotti remodeled them to suit his needs. He chose to do as little demolition as possible and limited new construction to a few interior walls, a balcony, and a closet. Gregotti felt in no way inhibited by the grandeur of the palatial space he had acquired but neither did he feel compelled to gut totally and modernize it. Rather, he strove to keep the best of the refined architectural detailing and those spatial qualities that did not impinge on his own convenience. Where they did, he modified the spaces to provide for such things as the necessities of storage, organization, flow, and number of rooms.

1. In bold contrast to the old-world grandeur of an ornate vaulted ceiling of white stucco on a colored background and walls freshly painted an intense, glossy violet blue is the simple, classic modern furniture Gregotti chose for the dressing room—an Alvar Aalto dining table and stool and a Thonet clothes tree.

2. In the bathroom the play of form, style, and texture among a modern Italian wall lamp, an English-style turn-of-the-century wash basin, which was in the house before remodeling, and an ornate Mexican mirror with its large festive frame of hand-worked tin delights the eye.

3. The painted ceiling in the studio was so high that there was ample room to put in a balcony that serves as a library and guest room. The rich neoclassic designs in the ceiling have simply been washed clean rather than restored. The primary architectural feature of the room is the beautiful nineteenth-century iron spiral staircase with its perforated steps painted silver. Acting as a counterpoint to the lightness of the staircase

is a large posterlike decorative panel by Giosetta Fioroni.

4. In the bedroom the exquisite eighteenth-century iron bedstead, painted black, echoes the richness of the Mexican mirror in the adjoining bathroom. A late-nineteenth-century poster on the wall captures just the right mood of light-hearted sophistication.

5. Painted over the fireplace in the bedroom is a decoration by Giosetta Fioroni that has been developed with few color tones other than gold and silver. The wicker chairs are painted silver—a surprise that seems particularly appropriate to these regal surroundings, and works particularly well with the painting.

Photographs by Carla de Benedetti

161

1

2

3

4

Franco Tartaglino Mazzucchelli

This glossy, highly sophisticated apartment was created by combining and gutting two traditional apartments, one above the other, on the top two floors of an old palace in Milan. By adeptly using a sand color as an almost tranquilizing background—on the walls and in wall-to-wall carpeting—Franco Tartaglino Mazzucchelli focuses all attention on his spatial legerdemain and his playful juxtapositioning of rectilinear forms with circular ones. A new staircase, which connects the various zones of the apartment, acts as a kind of structural fulcrum that holds all the disparate elements in balance. The detailing in the staircase and the stair rail is impeccable; as, indeed, it is throughout the apartment.

1. In the living room, under the protective wing of the stairs, an intimate sitting area has been sequestered. Built-in leather banquettes fit neatly into a space defined by a change of level. The carpet flows upward to sheathe a shelf-bar; its lip detailing is similar to that on the stairs. A lighted niche displays a sculpture and a plant to optimum dramatic effect.

2. In an open, free-flowing section of the living room, columns are played off against changes in floor and wall levels to sustain a bold spatial tension. A wall-mounted storage unit picks up the line and color of the baseboards.

3. The entrance hall with its cavelike dark blue walls and vaulted ceiling makes the sudden transition into the light, clear open space beyond all the more exciting by way of contrast. A pair of classic armchairs by Le Corbusier act as discreet foils for the exuberant Italian wall lights.

4. In the dining room, floor lamps with their shades tilted upward at an angle are used to illuminate a series of lithographs by Patrick Heron. A black table and chairs harmonize with the shiny dark blue walls.

5. In the study an arc lamp reiterates the roundness of the sculpture by Carla Castelbarco and the table lamp in the game room

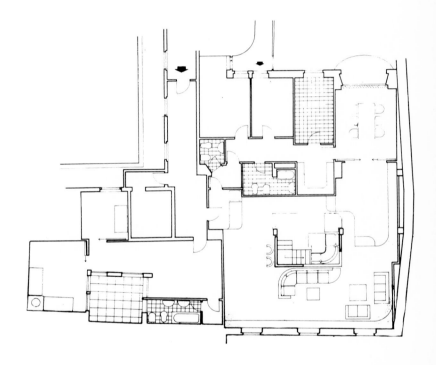

below. A tubular metal-and-glass table functions as a kind of stair rail around the perimeter of the open well.

Photographs by Carla de Benedetti

165

1 2

3 4

Acknowledgments

My special gratitude goes to Carla de Benedetti for her stunning photographs, her encouragement, and her friendship. I also wish to express my appreciation to Chris Holme for the handsome design of this book and to Bryan Holme for the enthusiasm and support he has given to all my book projects.

To my son, Christian, and to his most-perfect-of-all-nannies, Joan, go my love and my thanks for being so patient with me while I toiled mutely over my typewriter, and for making me laugh when I needed it most.